Praise for Sandra's *Choosing Happiness: Stories from Truly Happy People*

"I knew a few pages in I needed to get multiple copies to keep on my desk. I want not only the staff I work with but new employees that we on-board to receive this book so we can, as a team, reflect on how we bring happiness to work. The personal stories in this book brought focus to real life strategies that we all can relate to."

Deanna Villella
Manager of Employment Services
Job Gym, a division of the John Howard Society of Niagara

"Sandra has written a must-read book full of insightful information for those of us who want to learn about the benefits of choosing happiness at work. What I appreciated most was how Sandra captured the authenticity of the experiences shared by those she interviewed. This is a brilliant example of Sandra's passion for helping people become the best version of themselves."

Lori Watson
Director
Social Assistance & Employment Opportunities Niagara Region.

"Sandra has written a book that is a valuable tool for individuals, teams, and organizations who want to have a better way to communicate, collaborate and infuse general satisfaction in the workplace. The book includes real-life stories that are both inspirational and relatable. Sandra's optimistic and practical perspective shines through this refreshing approach to happiness in the workplace."

Robin L. Owens, Ph.D.
Leadership Purpose Coach, Founder
MASTERFUL Course Creations

"I have had the pleasure of knowing and working with Sandra for close to ten years. It is no surprise that she has authored a book on happiness. I love that her book reflects her values as much as it does those of whom she interviewed. Sandra has pulled together a practical guide; a book of ideas based on personal experiences, on how both the individual and the leader can contribute to a workplace where people are inspired to do good work."

Audie McCarthy
President & CEO
Mohawk College Enterprise

"Some of my fondest memories are the times Sandra and I would partner to design and deliver coaching sessions aimed at Leadership and Team Development. She is fun to partner with. She is bright and talented and competent. However, what puts Sandra over the top is that she always brings joy and laughter and comfort to her coaching. She makes you feel a happiness that you are sitting in her class and it is going to be a great day!"

Jack Grosvenor
President
jack grosvenor + associates

Choosing Happiness at Work

Stories from Truly Happy People

SANDRA SUMMERHAYES

Copyright © 2022 CLSR Inc. All rights reserved

Personality Dimensions is a Registered Trademark of Career/LifeSkills Resources Inc.

Myers-Briggs Type Indicator is a registered trademark of The Myers & Briggs Foundation in the United States and other countries

No part of this book may be reproduced, or stored in a retrieval system, or transmitted in any form or by any means, electronic, mechanical, photocopying, recording, or otherwise, without express written permission of the publisher.

Illustrations by: Chris Summerhayes

Published by:
CLSR Inc.
Aurora, ON L4G 3V7
www.clsr.ca

Library and Archives Canada Cataloguing in Publication

Title: Choosing happiness at work / Sandra Summerhayes.

Names: Summerhayes, Sandra, author.

Identifiers: Canadiana (print) 20220217343 | ISBN 9781894422611 (softcover)

Subjects: LCSH: Job satisfaction.

Classification: LCC HF5549.5.J63 S86 2022 | DDC 650.1—dc23

Acknowledgements

To the wonderful individuals who allowed me to interview them for this book, thank you for freely sharing your personal stories, ideas, and thoughts with me. It was a joy to hear so many unique perspectives on owning and creating happiness in the workplace. I'm grateful for your time and grateful that others may benefit in their own happiness journey from your experiences.

To my phenomenal editor Celia Carr, thank you for bringing my thoughts and ideas to life on the pages of this book.
To CLSR Inc., thank you for graciously publishing my first book. It has been a privilege working with you and I'm thrilled at the prospect of how many people we can encourage to find happiness through this partnership.

And finally, to my incredible husband Chris - I can't express how much it means to me that whenever I ask you, "do you think I can do this?" without hesitation, your response is always "of course you can". Thank you for your unending confidence and support in everything I do and a special thank you for your brilliant illustrations in this book.

CONTENTS

Acknowledgments	i
Introduction	1
About the book	5
One Size does not fit all	7
The freedom to fly	17
Keep the bigger picture in mind	25
A prescription for happiness	33
Prioritizing your happiness	41
Work as a safe space to land	49
Being a positive leader	57
Remember that life is good	65
Own it, work it and live it	73
Serve others with a smile	81
Final thoughts	89
About the author	93

Introduction

I absolutely love my job. I truly do.

You may be thinking, "Well, of course you love your job. You work for yourself." Self-employment does play a significant role in my overall happiness, but it does not show the full picture.

I have always been a happy person, both personally and professionally, which is partially why I was inspired to write this book in the first place. That is not to say that finding my calling happened overnight, nor did it happen in any ordinary way. Doing a job that I love came by taking advantage of opportunities presented to me throughout my life and by learning from several challenges.

That journey brought me to where I am now – completely and totally happy at work.

So much of my work revolves around helping people to be the

best version of themselves that this has been a wonderful opportunity for me to also reflect on my own happiness, what drives me, and how I maintain that happiness in my day-to-day. I do not wish to give the impression that every day is perfect, but I am adept at snapping myself out of the low points, and consciously working towards ensuring that things get better. For me, it is making the choice every day as to whether I will choose to be happy, and I hope through this book that I can encourage others to make that decision for themselves.

The value of being happy at work cannot be overstated. We spend too much of our time at work to not be happy while we are there. When we are not happy at work, it will inevitably spread to our personal lives, which in turn affects those around us. From a leadership perspective, when you are happy, your employees will be happy because you are role-modeling the behaviour you hope to see in others.

I am so inspired by each of the people I spoke to who are featured in the following pages. They are all positive and take it upon themselves to remain engaged by keeping other members of their team happy. The interviewees all come from different careers, are from different levels of management, and at different points in their career. Some are individuals I have known for years and have had the pleasure of working with throughout my own career, and some were recommended to me by their own loved ones for being so exceptionally happy at their jobs. In every case, they bring their own unique philosophies on what it means to be happy, and how to maintain that happiness in the workplace. I have been able to take these unique perspectives and put them to use in my own happiness development.

In putting this book together, more than ever, I believe that happiness at work is different for each person and that there requires an understanding that team members are individuals who are made happy for varying reasons. Leaders need to ask, "How can I make my team happy? How can I achieve happiness in my workplace?" For me, happiness is correlated to my ability to work with people, help others, and have others in my life who can help me. Every day, I am grateful to be in a position where I get to meet so many unique individuals who are eager for my knowledge but who are also able to teach me new lessons on life and happiness. I hope that everyone finds something in this book that resonates and sets them on a path toward achieving happiness more often and more abundantly.

About the Book

In April of 2019, I was on a cruise to Bermuda, Cape Canaveral and the Bahamas. The cruise line had people spraying our hands with sanitizer on our way into the buffet area. They were referred to as the "washy, washy, happy, happy" people because that is what they say to you as they spray your hands. What might have been considered an otherwise monotonous job to some was given a different approach on this particular cruise. The "washy, washy, happy, happy" people working that morning were named August and Red. August played the guitar while Red sang. They performed the Beatles song "I Want to Hold Your Hand" rewritten to reflect why they were sanitizing our hands. They did the same thing with Neil Diamond's "Sweet Caroline". They were having a ball and the customers were equally amused.

As my husband and I sat by the pool later that day, we reflected on breakfast and the performance put on by August and Red. I realized that while thinking back on my career, I could only count on the fingers of my two hands the number of people I have met that were truly happy at their jobs. I asked my husband, "wouldn't it be great if I could interview them so I could share their ideas with others who want to find happiness at work?" The rest is history.

The people I interviewed and whose experiences I've shared in this book come from all different industries, experiences and levels of employment. These are people that I have found, and who agree to be, genuinely happy in their jobs.

ONE SIZE DOES NOT FIT ALL
Encourage a collaborative work culture
- Andy's story -

Since 2012, I have been facilitating training sessions for a local training organization. We do what is called an open seat cohort that allows any company to participate in the course. The program is an eight-day leadership training course that takes place over the course of eight months, during which I get to know the participants quite well.

Day five of the program involves a leadership panel. During one of the sessions, Andy Broadbent, the Chief Financial Officer for a chain of greenhouse and gardening centres, was on the panel being interviewed and I recognized immediately how personable he was with everyone. He was as energized and as motivated as any of the other members of his staff. While I was reflecting on ideas for this book, and what happiness means in the workplace, Andy instantly came to mind. I was eager to learn more about what he does to stay happy, as well as what the company does to keep their employees excited about their jobs.

"You need to have balance in your role."

"To be happy at work, I think you need to be in an industry that you believe in. I think there has to be some consistency with your own personal values. You need to be in a place where communication is respected, both upwards and downwards. If you do have a voice, it needs to be heard but with the understanding that having it heard and changes being made are two different things. There also needs to be a combination of being in your comfort zone while also facing some new challenges. I think if you're 100 percent in your comfort zone, you're going to get bored fairly quickly, but I also believe that throwing someone in the deep end without the knowledge or skillset will stress them quickly, leading to unhappiness. You need to have balance in your role."

Andy is originally from Nova Scotia where he went to St. Mary's University in Halifax. From there he pursued his Chartered Accountant designation and begrudgingly ended up at a firm in Northern New Brunswick. Though the move to New Brunswick was met with reluctance, Andy says it is the best thing that could have happened to him at the time; he found a great group of friends and lived there for three years before being transferred back to Halifax for a year.

After meeting his wife, she and Andy moved to Bermuda where he spent the next ten years working in financial services. Though they enjoyed their time in Bermuda and still very much miss it, they decided when their children came of school age that it was time to return to Canada, choosing Ontario as their destination. Andy took a planned sabbatical, which extended longer than planned due to the economic crash in 2008. While on a job search, anticipating that he would be commuting to and from Toronto in a financial services role, Andy was eventually presented with an opportunity at the company where he has been ever since. "This job came up out of the blue which was only 15 minutes from where I live and required some of my skillsets. At the time, I don't think I, or the ownership group here, necessarily thought this would be an ongoing relationship, but it's been twelve years and it's going well. Some of getting here was by plan, but a lot of it has been luck. It's funny when you look back to figure out why things work out the way they do, and sometimes it's through no design at all. I said "no" to a few things and few things said "no" to me to get me where I am today."

> ***"The better the work culture is, the less likely it is that people will leave."***

"There's huge value in bringing happiness to the workplace, and it absolutely plays a role in employee retention. I don't think anyone is here because we're paying more than anyone else – I think if they decided they wanted to make more money, they could leave tomorrow and likely make a bit more. There must be other factors besides the compensation package, and I think we see that benefit here. Between the fees for online job postings and the time it takes to go through resumes, you are lucky to be able to find five candidates that may be suitable. You spend thousands of dollars just to fill entry level positions, and there's no guarantee that on day one, the person you've hired is the person they've said they are on their resume or in their interviews. The better the work culture is, the less likely it is that people will leave. You save on turnover costs which eventually flows through to the customer experience; happier, more experienced staff are better at dealing with good customers, and even more importantly, difficult customers. Brick-and-mortar retail isn't the highest grossing industry at the moment, so every little bit helps."

> *"We figure if they're happy, then they're going to make our customers happy as well."*

During our training sessions, one thing that I've noticed consistently is that participants from this company are always phenomenal. They are continually good-natured and eager to learn. They will always apply what they've learned every month and report back in the following session about their experience. They work exceptionally hard in the training classes and are both happy and motivated whenever I see them. Andy shared with me a bit about the culture that they have fostered for their employees, and much of it relies on the environment in which staff are working. Andy believes that the high morale is because most of the staff spends a significant portion of their workday outdoors. "I am not in that 98 percent, but in speaking to those who are, especially those who have been career-long retail employees, most tell me they could never go back to an indoor setting. The fresh air, even on a rainy day, makes the workday a little less dreary. Having the ability to go in and out, especially in the spring or summer, I think has a lot to do with happiness."

The culture of a workplace is also critical in determining how a workplace functions, and as Andy suggests, their company encourages a collaborative work culture so that employees are welcomed to contribute ideas to improve the company and the way they work. "I don't think we're the only company that says we're collaborative, but we genuinely listen to what our employees have to say. We might ask all our employees what five things they would like to see changed, and sometimes we honestly can't make all of those changes, but often times there's something suggested that we've been thinking about as well. If our employees feel the same way, then clearly a change needs to be made."

Rather than micromanage every location, Andy, and the rest of the executive team, believes in giving their location managers as much autonomy as possible, while ensuring the managers have the resources required to maintain their employees' happiness. Andy said that this is often something as simple as popsicles on a hot day, to sales contests or incentive prizes for employees that are doing good work. "We meet as a senior management group on a quarterly basis, and we make sure our location managers are here and at least once or twice per year, staff happiness is a main issue on the agenda. This time is used to ask what things we've done that have worked, as well as the things that haven't. With retention and turnover rates the way that they are, it's important to us. We figure if they're happy, then they're going to make our customers happy as well."

The team also recognizes that the workplace is an ever-changing enigma that must adapt to the needs of the employees "Our procedures manual is a living document. We don't leave it on the shelf to collect dust until we need it if we're being audited. It's something that is changing all the time because our employees are changing, our customers are changing and the company has to change with them."

> **"I believe that if it's not working out, it would probably be time to move on."**

"I believe that I am very much responsible for my own happiness. If I wasn't happy here, then I probably wouldn't be here and I wouldn't blame or put that responsibility on my boss, the ownership group or anyone else. I believe that if it's not working out, it would probably be time to move on."

Andy's resume includes a CA firm, an insurance broker as well as a start-up that was eventually publicly traded. Through his various experiences, Andy has faced no shortage of challenges and pressures, but when I asked if there was ever a time where he found himself unhappy at work, he said no. By and large, Andy's been lucky and has yet to find himself in a position where he felt the urgent need to get out of a work situation except once. This outlying experience taught Andy the importance of trusting your gut when vetting an employer or job opportunity. "There was an experience years ago where I ended up somewhere and quickly realized it was not a fit. I was there for a matter of days and I knew throughout the recruitment process that it was wrong for me but decided to ignore what I was hearing. I don't think they necessarily did anything wrong, but I knew it wasn't for me. I've been fortunate in my career that I've always worked for great organizations, and great, caring people. That's not to say it's all been a bed of roses, but I can't think of a time where I was incredibly unhappy."

> *"I hope that if I left, they would be disappointed, but ready to continue making improvements."*

"I like leaving things in a better way than they were found. I don't want to be disrespectful because it assumes that maybe I found things already in a bad place but that's not necessarily the case. The ownership group here is fantastic. They give us the freedom and the resources to do what we need to do our jobs, but if I left tomorrow, I think both my boss and I would say that we have and would continue to have a great relationship. I hope that if I left, they would be disappointed, but ready to continue making improvements."

> *"There's always areas where we can do better or that we may not have the knowledge in right now to even know that we should be doing better. I don't think that ever really stops in a workplace."*

"I think you need to listen to your teams and find out what's really important to them outside of work. People are always going to appreciate a raise, but there might be something simple like leaving early on Fridays. Maybe 20 and 30 years ago, work hours were work hours and life needed to be built around your work life, but now, good organizations have recognized that life has changed. Maybe it's having flex time available or allowing someone to bring their child to work if their childcare fell through that day. Rather than create a more stressful situation for employees, ask how you can create an easier situation. It's a win-win for everyone because that person is going to go home happy that they were able to leave early or not have to book a day off because of their childcare. With my accountant's hat on, it's almost like a return-on-investment."

"I want to make sure we know that we've still got a long way to go. There's always areas where we can do better or that we may not have the knowledge in right now to even know that we should be doing better. I don't think that ever really stops in a workplace. Where I was before, work came first, second and third and family came fourth. That's just the way it was, and when you took the job, it wasn't hidden from you. I'm still in touch with people from that firm and it's clear that dynamic has had to change because they realized they can't expect people to work 15-hour days and wonder where people are on Saturdays. When my first child was born, I got a work call not an hour after he was born, and that was a Sunday night. Those things change over time, and we are nowhere near perfect, but the key is that we recognize that change is necessary. We listen as much as possible and unfortunately, sometimes, we have to say no, but we always explain why. We would love to give everyone eight weeks of vacation, but that's not going to work from a coverage perspective. We keep it in mind and recognize that one person might prefer more time off than a massive raise. Everyone is driven by different things, so to understand that one size does not fit all puts you ahead of the curve."

THE FREEDOM TO FLY
Discover what makes you tick
- *Marylou's story* -

I was introduced to Marylou Hilliard through a mutual connection while I was working on a contract through an organization for employment services. The woman who made the connection knows us both quite well and knew that we would be an excellent fit for one another. I contacted Marylou and we met for a coffee at a nice little café in Ridgeville, near Marylou's home. We had a wonderful conversation, and it didn't take long for us both to realize how much we have in common; we have similar values and found out that we're the same personality type according to the Myers-Briggs Type Indicator®.

When Marylou found out that I am also a Laughter Coach, she told me about a Wellness Conference she was facilitating and asked me if I would be one of the keynote speakers. After that conference, we both knew we wanted to continue our working relationship.

Marylou moved to the Niagara Region from Toronto. She lives in Fonthill and has very quickly become involved in her community. What I admire most about Marylou is her tenacity, not only for herself but for others. She does a lot for her community and works equally hard in her volunteer efforts as she does in her professional endeavors. If she's passionate about it, she puts in everything and is happy to do so.

> *"If you get up every morning and want to go to work, then that's happiness."*

"Happiness at work is whatever ignites your passion, or whatever gets you up in the morning and makes you look forward to your day. It's being motivated to continue to make things happen. It doesn't matter whether you're someone with a strict routine or have a different schedule every day, if you get up every morning and want to go to work, then that's happiness."

> *"I love hearing something, remembering someone else with similar interests and being able to connect those two people. It makes me happy to ignite that spark."*

"I think I'm very happy at work. I would say I'm generally quite happy most of the time. I'd be lying if I said I was always happy, but I would say that I am at least 80 percent of the time, and it's because I know what makes me happy. What makes me happy is having the freedom to fly, having a lot of great ideas and getting up each day, never having the day repeat itself. I love unusual ideas and connecting people. I love hearing something, remembering someone else with similar interests and being able to connect those two people. It makes me happy to ignite that spark."

Growing up watching fictional advertising tycoon Darrin Stephens on the television show *Bewitched*, Marylou was drawn to advertising from an early age. She says she has been critiquing ads for as long as she can remember and that from about the age of 12, she made it her mission to prepare for a career in advertising. Her rigorous work ethic began when she started at a grocery store at the age of 13 for the sole purpose of saving for college. The college on which she set her sights, and did in fact attend, had a 95 percent placement rate with various Toronto agencies. She hitchhiked to school for three years before landing an internship that turned into a job during her third year of study. The position was as a media estimator. Although Marylou found this particular job boring, she was nonetheless thrilled to have officially entered the field of advertising.

From there, she was offered a position at an agency where she met a mentor who showed her everything from finance to production to strategy. For three more years, Marylou worked hard during the day while studying at night to eventually earn the coveted Gold Medal and Certified Advertising Practitioner Certificate.

Marylou went on to work at a few more agencies, travelling the world for global meetings as a representative for several Fortune 500 companies and a host of other global organizations.

Eventually Marylou decided that she wanted to return to her roots by working more closely with clients and it was at this point that she opened HG Communications. She was fortunate to have a former client back her decision, remaining loyal to Marylou until there was a change of client management. Marylou believes she has always been an entrepreneur at heart with advertising in her DNA. She loves what she does and says that it never feels like work, rather that she gets "paid to play."

> ***"I think self-awareness is a big part of finding happiness."***

"You have to find out what makes you tick. A lot of people don't know what makes them tick. I'm fortunate enough that I do. I've had the luxury of taking a lot of personal assessments, so I had a pretty solid idea of what made me happy. Time after time, I would get the results back from these personality assessments, all with very similar profiles of who I am, what motivates me and what makes me happy. It was very validating because it was almost like when each one came back and was painting the same picture, it made me very self-aware. I think self-awareness is a big part of finding happiness.

I think happiness is a combination of doing things mindfully and being innate. I've always been a naturally happy person, but when I find that I'm not happy, I'm able to step back to assess what's holding me back, and what it is that's making me feel off my game."

> ***"You can't be creative if you're not happy. If you're down, or being held back by something, you can't reach new ideas or the kind of thinking you need to be creative."***

"If I'm in a situation where something is making me unhappy, only I can change it. I can either address the situation and try to adjust it, or I can leave. I have the luxury of working with people I choose to work with, and that makes a huge difference. If someone was making me unhappy, I would change positions. I would change the job. I can resign clients. I can choose not to work for people I don't want to work for."

During our discussion, Marylou recalled a time in her career where she was unhappy, but that she allowed herself to stay in the situation longer than she should have. Her employer lacked interpersonal skills, often saying things at inappropriate times. Though Marylou said it was hard not to take it personally at first, eventually she was able to rise above the issue until she was able to depart from that environment. She says to be in a creative role like she is in, happiness is imperative. "You can't be creative if you're not happy. If you're down, or being held back by something, you can't reach new ideas or the kind of thinking you need to be creative."

> *"I tell them to write what makes them happy and what doesn't because sometimes it's in the things you don't like where you can find what you do like, and that will make you happy."*

"This may not be right for everyone, but my suggestion is to journal. I'm also a certified coach practitioner, so when people come to me and say they're just floundering around, I tell them that they should journal. Try to find a place where you can really have some peace of mind and let the thoughts flow freely. I tell them to write what makes them happy and what doesn't because sometimes it's in the things you don't like where you can find what you do like, and that will make you happy. If I were to describe in just a few words what makes me the happiest, it's having the freedom to fly. When I feel that freedom is going to be taken away, I feel blocked. This can happen through someone being negative or sending negative energy. If someone is sending negative energy my way, I can feel it, the same way I can feel when positive energy is being sent my way."

> *"We put people into the workforce and expect them to work 9 to 5, or longer, and be accountable for every hour that's put in. It's just very counterintuitive to me."*

"An example of having the freedom to fly is having a potential contract and they expect me to be somewhere from 9 to 5 every day. I always say, you go through school and when you start in kindergarten you get some freedom. Yes, you're in class for a certain length of time but they've got freedom to play and have fun. Then you get to elementary school and you've got boundaries – you have to be there for a set amount of time and they start to suck the creativity out of you. There have been studies where they've gone into classrooms and asked first grade students if they feel they are creative. Most of them will raise their hands. By grade four or so, only about a quarter of the students will raise their hands because they're already starting to pigeonhole themselves by saying, 'I'm scientific', or 'I'm this', 'I'm that'. Then you get into high school, and you get a little bit more freedom. You can skip classes and there may be consequences, but you can get away with doing it. Then you get to college and university and you've really got freedom. You attend the classes, or you don't, and there's no consequences other than that you need to keep up with your work. Then we put people into the workforce and expect them to work 9 to 5, or longer, and be accountable for every hour that's put in. It's just very counterintuitive to me."

"It makes me really happy when I am meeting with someone, and I can connect them to somebody else who is going to help their cause."

"I think helping other people to find their passion and to be happy in what they do makes me happy. I'm a connector, and time after time, personality assessments come back and tell me that I'm the explorer-promoter, so that's one badge I've been given. Intuitive connector is another. It makes me really happy when I am meeting with someone and I can connect them to somebody else who is going to help their cause."

I am one of those fortunate people that has been able to make a connection with Marylou, and we've been able to work on some exciting things as a result. As Marylou says, "we ignite each other's passion".

KEEP THE BIGGER PICTURE IN MIND
Setting yourself up for success
- Joseph's story -

When I was studying happiness in the workplace and searching for individuals who are especially positive about their careers, it was important to me that I included a cross-section of people from different lines of work, but also at different points in their career. I was having trouble finding younger people who I felt were particularly passionate about what they do, until I was introduced to Joseph Beiner.

I was working with a contract writer on some content for my website and when I told her about my book idea, she insisted I speak with her fiancé, Joseph, who has spent the better part of a decade working in construction. She told me she has never met anyone else who not only enjoys work, but is excited to go every day, especially in a career that is so physically demanding. I met Joseph for a coffee and was instantly impressed by his outlook on life and his philosophy on happiness in the workplace.

> *"No matter what, if I'm having a bad day, I can think about what I want and that way, my life goals never feel too far out of reach; it feels like I'm doing the right thing."*

"I think happiness at work is, for the most part, a mindset. It's not always about being happy in the here and now because there will always be days that are grey and gloomy. I think when I really became happy and was embracing my work was when I started thinking about my future. No matter what, if I'm having a bad day, I can think about what I want and that way, my life goals never feel too far out of reach; it feels like I'm doing the right thing. I can get through any of the other issues because I know I'm doing the right things to get me to where I want to be."

Joseph realized his passion for construction while working for an above ground pool company as a summer job while he was attending college. It was only his first construction job, but it did not take long for him to transition from being a labourer to building entire pools. He was attending College in Peterborough at the time for Child and Youth Studies, and while he initially loved the idea of working with children, that summer solidified his desire to work in construction. When Joseph returned to College in the fall, he switched to a construction skills program.

Early in the academic year, Joseph was forced to take time away from his studies when he became ill. This quickly caused his grades to slip at which point he had to make the difficult decision to drop out of the program. He moved back home in Niagara where he started working for his stepfather's residential construction company. Though the circumstances for the transition were not ideal, it ended up being the best thing that could have happened. "I felt like a huge failure at the time – I did for quite a while because I couldn't really see the big picture. I worked with my stepdad for four years, just living day-by-day. I always planned on going back to school, because I didn't know what I wanted to do. My stepdad laid out a path for me that I didn't see at the time, but the more I did it, the better I got and realized that I really enjoyed working in construction."

After four years of working in exterior renovations with his stepdad, Joseph was eager to learn more and decided to move to a bigger Niagara-based commercial and residential construction company. He took a significant pay cut by switching, but he spent another three years working for this company before finally landing a carpenter job with another major construction company which, in his words, is the best thing that has happened to him.

"When I am feeling down, I tend to set my mind straight and put myself into the task at hand, embrace the good and forget the bad."

"It's one of those things where you can't have one without the other. I care for others, so I tend to be a listener which I think is important because people want to be heard. Also, for me to be as positive as I am, I think it rubs off on others which creates a more positive environment for me to thrive. Even though I'm helping others, I'm setting myself up to have a good day. When I am feeling down, I tend to set my mind straight and put myself into the task at hand, embrace the good and forget the bad."

"I think that's what it means to be a leader – walking that line and setting the tone while remaining humble. People feed off that."

"I think if you're happy, it brings out confidence, and those two things combined with passion make for excellent leadership skills. People tend to look up to those who are happy and confident at work which is what companies look for and want to build on. When I'm at work and there's someone that I don't get along with, which is rare, but it happens, I try to remain positive. I'm there to do my job because at the end of the day, I want to have set myself up if there's a promotion or new opportunity. I don't want to give anyone a reason to not give that to me; you have to be methodical in your approach to setting yourself up for success. I don't think you can have admiration without judgement. I think people tend to be envious of those they admire, but with that I like to think comes motivation. I think that's what it means to be a leader – walking that line and setting the tone while remaining humble. People feed off that."

> ***"It's important to always set yourself up for success. Bet on yourself. It can be scary sometimes, but the risk is worth the reward."***

"I'm committed and the good always outweighs the bad. I think for the most part, I'm a pretty happy person and I think that when you set yourself up for success and you try to always push yourself, you're likely going to be a more positive person. Instead of getting down or letting the small things weigh on you, you think about the big picture, and it tends to get you through."

When I asked Joseph who he felt was responsible for his happiness at work, his response was that he needed to take responsibility for his own actions, decisions and of course, his own happiness. Joseph is working on large construction projects including highways and overpasses but continues to do smaller exterior renovation projects on the side. His philosophy has always been that he would never do anything to someone's home that he wouldn't do to his own, including cutting corners to get the job done faster or using cheap products. "Even if you're not in a great work environment, or not in a great job and you're getting paid less than what you feel you deserve, you're still the one putting your name on your work. Just because you feel there may not be other opportunities available right now, it doesn't mean that opportunities won't come, so it's important to always set yourself up for success. Bet on yourself. It can be scary sometimes, but the risk is worth the reward."

> *"Even if it's at a slower pace, I'm going to do it right every time. Eventually I'll get faster, but I'd rather get faster doing the work the right way."*

"Always keep the big picture in mind. Set goals, make them attainable, and when you get there, start over; set new goals and move forward. As for the company - make sure your employees feel heard, and don't be afraid to give someone a pat on the back when they deserve it. Also, people tend to give you the level of work and level of themselves that you are paying for. I have found that companies don't seem to understand the big picture when setting wages for their employees, but if you pay them a little bit more, the upfront cost may be more, but you are going to get something in return for that. Where I work, I feel I'm overpaid but actually it's just because we're getting paid properly for the work we do, so I try to push myself to do the absolute best that I can. People will say to me, "we're not building a church – it doesn't have to be perfect," but if the company is willing to pay me to do this level of work, I want to do the best that I can. Even if it's at a slower pace, I'm going to do it right every time. Eventually I'll get faster, but I'd rather get faster doing the work the right way."

> *"Only you can know what you need to make yourself happy."*

"I like to think of that movie *Pay it Forward*; if my happiness rubs off on a hundred people, and even just one of those people can build off of that in some small way, I'm doing my part as a human to make the world a better place. Again, we all need to see the bigger picture. It's okay to live day-to-day and enjoy the small moments, but if you're happy where you are, and you want to continue to be happy, you have to set yourself up."

It can be incredibly difficult to maintain happiness in a career when you're in a workplace that doesn't appreciate what you have to offer and speaking to Joseph made me wonder how many people have left careers entirely because of one negative job experience. We should all demand happiness for ourselves, and sometimes that means finding it in unconventional ways. It's okay to go to school for one career and end up in another, just as it's okay to use a job as a steppingstone to get to where you want to be. Not every day is going to be perfect, but we owe it to ourselves to see beyond our day-to-day lives and envision what we want for ourselves so that we can grow toward it. "Only you can know what you need to make yourself happy. The world is an amazing place, and it can be scary to take risks in your career, but if you're not happy, take the risk. Always set yourself up as best as you can and bet on yourself."

A PRESCRIPTION FOR HAPPINESS
The importance of maintaining work-life balance
- *Christina's story* -

I was speaking with my very good friend Tony about my idea to interview exceptionally happy people to write a book focused on happiness in the workplace. Without hesitation he said, "oh, my goodness, you have to interview Christina."

Christina Ciancio is Tony's niece, and a pharmacy entrepreneur. She was previously a pharmacist at a larger company but when things were no longer working out, she and one of her colleagues decided to branch out on their own and opened a small pharmacy in Thorold, Ontario. While I was speaking with Christina, the focus that their pharmacy places on customer service and employee satisfaction was abundantly clear. They love working in a smaller, less rigid environment, where they know everyone who comes into their store. She also said the switch to owning her own business has improved her family's happiness because her children get to spend more time with their mother. You can tell how much family means to her and how having that balance has influenced her happiness in the workplace.

> *"There are still stresses, as with any job, but I don't feel like I dread having to go to work. I feel like I no longer bring all the stresses home with me or carry it throughout the day."*

"When I was reflecting on how happy I am at work, I asked my children, 'is mommy different now? Do you like it better with mommy working at the new place?' Caitlin, at the age of seven, said 'well you don't sell toys at this pharmacy mommy'. Well, no, we don't, but I came from a place where we did sell toys, but I was working long hours. We were open at eight in the morning which means I would be out of the house by 7:30 and sometimes working until 10 at night. There were days where I didn't even see my children because they were still asleep when I left and asleep when I returned home. Sometimes we do have long hours at the new pharmacy because it's ours, so we need to be there a lot, but we have more control over balancing our work with our home lives. There are still stresses, as with any job, but I don't feel like I dread having to go to work. I feel like I no longer bring all the stresses home with me or carry it throughout the day. I don't feel miserable in my home life and my anxiety has declined greatly."

Born and raised in Thorold, Ontario, Christina Ciancio knew from a young age that she would pursue a career in healthcare. When she was in high school, she landed a job at a local pharmacy which helped shape her interest in becoming a pharmacist. She continued working at the local pharmacy for the next four years while completing her undergraduate degree in Health Sciences at Brock University. She spent another four years in pharmacy school at the University of Toronto, and when she returned, began working at the same local pharmacy in Thorold as a licensed pharmacist for the next ten years. Eventually, Christina was given more responsibility as the designated manager, a role she held for nearly four years. She had her two children during her time at the pharmacy which began changing her expectations of what she wanted from work.

In 2018, the owner of the pharmacy was planning to sell the business, so Christina, and her colleague Alexandra, put in an offer. They were not the successful bidder. "At this point we were presented with a fork in the road. We could stay, but it looked like it was going to be a corporate store with a much more rigid structure, or there was another owner to come in with a lot more quotas and targets to meet. Our other option was to branch out on our own."

After exploring a few options and determining what it would mean for them both financially and personally, Christina and Alexandra are now business partners and have opened their own pharmacy.

> *"We try to make sure everyone gets the right training for the jobs they're doing so that they feel fulfilled."*

"I feel like people need to be recognized. Everybody has their own set of strengths and weaknesses, so for people to work to the best of their abilities, they need to be able to build a set of skills and have tasks around those strengths and weaknesses. If everyone is contributing and doing something that they enjoy, and that they feel they are trained well to do, that will make them feel motivated and happier. If they don't feel as though they've been trained well enough, they're not going to feel comfortable in that position. For that reason, we try to make sure everyone gets the right training for the jobs they're doing so that they feel fulfilled. We make sure they feel recognized and that they know when they're doing a great job, because when people don't feel valued, they're unlikely to care about their job.

Taking time from work, and taking breaks is also important, even if you're in an environment that makes you happy. When I was in a situation where I wasn't as happy as I am now, I would try to find at least one patient each day that I could really connect with so that I knew I was making a difference in at least one person's life. That energy was enough to get me through any of the bad things that might happen in a day."

Christina also believes that happiness comes internally, and that people need to find their own self-motivation in order to be truly happy. She said it's also about the team you have in place and that it is helpful when everyone is working on the same page, toward the same goals.

> ***"To be able to practice the way we want to practice, and to be able to do what we went to school to do without the corporate mentality, this is for us. It's our vision that we get to realize and work towards."***

When Christina began telling people that she and Alexandra were planning on opening their own pharmacy, they were met with worry and confusion. Christina recalls telling a colleague, who was going to be the new owner of the pharmacy where she was working, that she would be leaving. "Why would you do that? You're never going to make as much money as you would have been making here," was his reply. Christina said that although that was true, the trade-offs have been worth the dip in pay: "We feel we are providing better care to our patients here. We don't feel as rushed. We don't feel pressured to meet a certain target or quota. We're able to focus on the needs of our customers, which is a really nice feeling." She says that it has also been worth it to spend more time with her family, and to have a more inviting environment in which to work. "To be able to practice the way we want to practice, and to be able to do what we went to school to do without the corporate mentality, this is for us. It's our vision that we get to realize and work towards."

Christina learned that she and Alexandra were not alone in wanting to break free from the corporate pharmacy life. "I have another friend that was in one of my pharmacy classes and she is doing the same thing. We didn't know because we both had to be secretive about our plans and then one day, she told me, 'I'm opening a pharmacy,' and I said, 'no way! I'm opening a pharmacy!' It was a very similar situation and she just opened her pharmacy too. She also came from a larger pharmacy and values having not only the independence but the ability to have more balance in her life."

> *"Some employers can be very generous with their benefit programs, but I think with this new shift, people are looking for more than just incentives at work."*

"The value in workplace happiness is huge. We spend so much of our time in our work environments, sometimes more than we spend in our home. I think there's been a huge shift in the culture of work, especially in North America to find happiness at work and in general. I think it's imperative that we're happy at work because it's where we spend so much time.

I do feel that sometimes people don't see or understand that value. It might be an 'old school' mentality, and they haven't bought into the idea that people should be happy at work. I've experienced it in places where I've previously worked. We tried to talk about employee incentive programs that would reward people, or just recognize them for the great things they were doing, but they were not interested. They didn't see the value. Some employers can be very generous with their benefit programs, but I think with this new shift, people are looking for more than just incentives at work."

> *"We want to continue the vision to have the best patient care and we want the patients to see that we value them as well as our staff."*

"We are hoping to expand our business. We don't have a terribly large staff right now, but I can see it now with the patients that are coming in that we are enjoying ourselves at work. I think that's a huge part of what draws people in. I hope that the feeling we have fostered here will continue to grow as we get more employees. We want to continue the vision to have the best patient care and we want the patients to see that we value them as well as our staff."

> *"If you bring happiness to work, others will feed off that and eventually, patients, as well as other team members, will follow suit. That happiness will continue to grow."*

"Don't give up. Sometimes it can be a struggle to build happiness in work environments. There may always be team members who don't want to get on board even when management is on board. If morale is low, keep pushing and make sure you're leading by example. If you bring happiness to work, others will feed off that and eventually, patients, as well as other team members, will follow suit. That happiness will continue to grow."

Leaving the stability of a job to pursue opening your own business can be incredibly terrifying, but if your current job is inhibiting you from being happy in other parts of your life then it may be time to re-evaluate. That is exactly what Christina did and she has never been happier.

PRIORITIZING YOUR HAPPINESS
Bring your passion into your work
- Paul's story -

Paul Copcutt is a marketing consultant with a specialized focus on personal branding. We met in 2005 when I was coordinating a two-day leadership conference where he was one of my concurrent workshop leaders. As I was listening to him speak, my immediate thought was that I needed to hire him to assist with my own personal branding. At the time, I found I was attending far too many networking events and doing a lot of one-off training sessions. I was spending too much time working without getting very much done. Another year went by and Paul ended up being at the conference again, this time as one of the keynote speakers. It was 2006 and finally, I made the wise decision to hire him.

The first thing Paul had me do was write a mission statement. This ended up being a tougher task than I anticipated because I had a habit of thinking I could do everything for everyone. He continued to probe and ask questions until finally, I became so frustrated, I said, "look, all I want to do is help leaders succeed!" to which Paul replied, "well, isn't that a great mission." "Helping leaders succeed" has been my mission statement ever since.

Paul has travelled an interesting road that has led him to his success as a personal branding specialist and he is genuinely great at what he does; he's excellent at brainstorming, coaching and is an all-around great person who has not only found his niche, but also exemplifies workplace happiness.

> *"I would say that most of the time my work is fulfilling. When it's not, I wouldn't say I'm less happy, but it might be that I'm not leveraging my unique capabilities."*

"To me, workplace happiness is doing work you're good at with like-minded people for clients with whom you enjoy spending time, because if you are self-employed, like myself, why take work that doesn't give you that? We can probably all find work that helps us to generate the revenue we want. We left corporate for a reason. Whatever that reason, why would you compromise that by working with people you don't enjoy being with or who don't share your values?"

Paul grew up in the United Kingdom and began his career in banking because, as his father said, "it's a job for life." It wasn't long before Paul realized he despised banking and transitioned into advertising sales for a newspaper. When he was 21, he applied for a job with a cigarette company doing sales in the UK. Eventually he went back into sales with a biotech company that eventually transferred him to Canada.

For Paul, there is an undeniable link between money and happiness, but only to a fairly small extent. "There are surveys out there that say once you make about $70,000 per year, you'll be happy, and I think that's an accurate figure. Once you have that, you can pay for most of what you need, and the rest is just gravy." A lot of people aspire for the six to seven figure business, but for Paul, once he reaches the amount where he's comfortable, he must be doing work he loves, otherwise it's not worth doing. "I would say that most of the time my work is fulfilling. When it's not, I wouldn't say I'm less happy, but it might be that I'm not leveraging my unique capabilities. If I find myself thinking, 'I can do this, but I don't really need to be doing this,' or, 'I don't like doing this,' then work becomes more of a chore than something I enjoy."

Paul previously believed in telling people to follow their passions for their career but has since changed his opinion because their passion may not be directly correlated to earning money. Now he believes in striking a balance by bringing more of what you're passionate about into your job. He spoke of a-workshop attendee of his who is an elementary school principal. "She loves film. She's a big film buff and she has an Oscars party every year. She brings a red carpet to her school on the first day of classes in September so that every new child has the chance to walk down the red carpet. The parents are invited to come and hold up signs while they cheer. One year, she had a kindergarten student who was too petrified to walk down the red carpet but an eighth-grade student bent down and said, 'come on, buddy, it'll be so much fun', and they walked down the red carpet together. She snapped a photo and sent it to me. I tell that story in all of my presentations now because all she did was bring a little bit of what she's passionate about and made it relevant to work."

> *"The biggest incentive for me starting my own business was being happy and working from home. My first child was also born so there was also some benefit there, but underlying, the reason was happiness."*

Paul can think of two distinct instances where work did not make him happy, and both for significantly different reasons. When Paul was 21 and working for the cigarette company, it was almost like a party where everything was paid for – company cars, hotel rooms five nights per week and their own expense accounts. The company eventually pulled out of the UK, making Paul and many of his colleagues redundant. Many of the employees struggled to find work afterwards, especially work that had a culture similar to the job they just lost. Paul eventually found a job with a car rental company, which was a short-lived career move. "I did it because it was a Central London sales rep job and I thought it would be fun, but because it was a rental car company, I could not mentally make the transition from selling a product to a service. I didn't enjoy it because I couldn't see a concrete result. It's ironic because that's what I do now, I sell a service, but back then I just couldn't do it."

The second instance where Paul found himself unhappy at work was with a recruiting company. The owner of the company put him on a team with two others who were already running the department. Paul's "teammates" immediately resented him as they had to split the sales three ways instead of two. They continually worked to undermine Paul in almost anything he did. He hated it but stuck it out for an extended period because the money was good. The last straw for Paul was when his colleagues unethically went behind his back and upset a client. "That was what pushed me towards working for myself. I joined another recruitment company for a short period of time and thought, 'You know what? I'm only going to be happy if I'm doing this myself because then I can decide how I want to do it.' The biggest incentive for me starting my own business was being happy and working from home. My first child was also born so there was also some benefit there, but underlying, the reason was happiness."

> *"I like having routines because they help me keep things in perspective and to keep things in check. They also help me to identify what I should be doing."*

Paul believes that while there are certain factors that will certainly contribute to increasing happiness, it also needs to be done mindfully. "I don't think it's necessarily innate in any of us to be happy or to help our employees be happy. Some people may do it subconsciously and it seems natural because it's one of their strengths, but I think people still have to be mindful that they're doing it."

Gratitude has also played a role in how Paul manages his happiness. When someone has done something to go above and beyond, he acknowledges and thanks them. "I think that's important because everyone wants to feel valued at work, whatever the work is." He also takes time at the end of each day to reflect and ask himself questions including. Did I do what I was supposed to do? What did I enjoy? What didn't I enjoy? What worked well? What didn't work well? How can I change that? How can I ensure I'm happier, or more productive, next week?

> ***"I think when someone feels valued in
> their job, no matter what kind of job it is,
> they will go the extra mile."***

"For me, being happy at work means feeling fulfilled, productive and like I'm making a difference. I think when someone feels valued in their job, no matter what kind of job it is, they will go the extra mile. My son, for example, is 19 and in the beginning stages of discovering what he wants to do. He's tried a few jobs and I can always tell where he's appreciated. He did a seasonal job with a cosmetics company which is such a great company to look at in terms of how they train and treat their employees. They gave everyone last Friday off so they could participate in the climate march. I see him come in from a day's work and can tell if he's had a good day because someone's recognized him. It isn't always necessarily a boss – it could be a colleague or a customer. You can see it lifts him when he talks about his day. As for whether happiness garners admiration or judgement, it could just be jealousy. They might not want to see others happy because they're not happy themselves."

"You can't expect other people to be responsible for your happiness at work or in life."

"There's a quote I've read that says, 'the only person who's responsible for your happiness is you'. I think the world of work has changed in the last 20 to 30 years. Previously in my career I would have expected my boss or manager to make life enjoyable for me at work, or to tell me what to do and check in on me to make sure that I'm happy. However, now I think the responsibility falls to us, because we're typically not with the same employer for life. People switch jobs, careers all the time. Managers leave. You can't expect other people to be responsible for your happiness at work or in life."

"Leaders should be brave enough to help employees find that happiness elsewhere."

"For leaders to build happy teams, I would say find out what happiness means to each individual and then work with them or as a team to achieve that. If it's not possible, leaders should be brave enough to help employees find that happiness elsewhere. I can think of a good example of a company that does this. Once they finish their training, they offer every employee $5,000 if they want to leave. It's an attractive amount of money because they only want people that are going to deliver, are happy and customer service focused.

Even if the person is stellar in training, they will still make the offer and if the person decides to take it and leave, the company sees that they saved themselves money in the long run."

> *"I think the driving factor behind what I do is helping people realize that what they do has value for others. I love it when people tell me they have a fantastic new job, they've been promoted, or they're finally being recognized if they haven't been before."*

For those looking for help with shaping their personal brand and rejuvenating the passion in what they do, Paul is certainly someone to know. It wasn't an easy or seamless road for him to get to where he is and find happiness in his work, but by going through several different roles and learning what did not make him happy, Paul has been able to find his own happiness and bring that to others looking to do the same.

WORK AS A SAFE SPACE TO LAND
Being both a cheerleader & a challenger
- *Fiona's story* -

Fiona Peacefull has always radiated happiness and positivity, so much so that her mother used to tell her that she was born laughing. This is why she was given the middle name Gay, a French word for "merry", a name that Fiona absolutely lives up to.

I met Fiona while facilitating a personality type workshop for the organization where she was employed. Years later, I submitted a proposal to design and deliver Managing Performance training at the government office where she happened to be the Training Coordinator. Working together closely that year, I quickly found Fiona to be one of the happiest, warmest, and most intuitive women I've had the pleasure of knowing.

Fiona began her career as a Career Counsellor. She eventually transitioned into the government sector, working in Human Resources and Public Health. She worked briefly as the HR Director for a municipality and is now the Director of People Services for the regional health system. I have been fortunate over the years to work with Fiona in both a professional as well as volunteer capacity, and she continues to be someone from whom I draw inspiration for her creative ideas and genuine positivity.

"Bringing your best self while helping others to do the same and having a direct correlation between the employee and customer experience, allows for true happiness to arc."

"I think being happy at work means that you can do your best while elevating others around you and making a difference for those you serve. My career has primarily been in government or not-for-profit roles and generally the people you serve are residents of the community or specific demographics. So for me, bringing your best self while helping others to do the same, and having a direct correlation between the employee and customer experience, allows for true happiness to arc."

> *"If you can create a space of safety for your employees, that's where I think people actually do their best work."*

"To me, happiness is the most critical element you can have in a workplace. There's so much pressure in our world and I think there are very few people who show up to the workplace who haven't experienced a hiccup before they get there. You need a safe space to land, and if it's not at work, it has to be home, or vice versa. If you can create a space of safety for your employees, that's where I think people actually do their best work."

> *"For me, bringing happiness into the workplace involves developing a sense of connection, and as a leader, building trust with employees by listening and giving them a voice."*

"Something I've always done when I've been accountable for supporting a team is walking around and saying good morning to everyone as soon as I've gotten myself organized in the morning. At one job, there were about 65 folks and I tried to be as visible a leader as possible by connecting with every individual and by understanding their work pressures and priorities.

I think people can truly be their best self when you know what makes them feel inspired, so besides just walking around to say good morning to whomever is there, it's knowing everyone's names, of course, but also knowing everyone's kids' names, their dogs' names, their spouses' names along with the interests they have outside of work. For me, bringing happiness into the workplace involves developing a sense of connection, and as a leader, building trust with employees by listening and giving them a voice. You've probably heard me say before to not mistake my kindness for stupidity, so once people can see that you want to genuinely connect, you allow them to make decisions and you enable them to move forward. You're not a barrier. I have always known that it's important to stand back; when someone in the room is smarter and knows more, let them shine. I love to talk, so it's a conscious effort, but it truly makes a difference. I, myself, have worked with people who stood behind me and really pushed me when they saw I was ready to be in front, and that has always made me happy."

> *"We often seek out a cheerleader before we seek out someone who is a challenger, and I think I've been lucky enough to have people who have been both."*

The notion that positivity does not always come in the form of having a constant cheerleader is something Fiona emphasizes when discussing happiness in the workplace. Being happy and being a positive influence in the workplace can still involve having tough conversations. Often, it's the gentle, but tough conversations that will have the most positive impact on an employee's production. One of Fiona's former employees told her, "you know, Fiona, you can tell me to go to hell and I'll look forward to the trip. You can challenge me, you can tell me that I didn't do something right, but in the end, I'm okay with it because you gave me the message in a way that didn't tear me down, didn't embarrass me, but lifted me up." Being happy doesn't need to always be overt and doesn't require grand gestures of positivity all the time. Sometimes it's just in the "good mornings," connecting with people, investing in your team through learning sessions, and in having intentional conversations that encourage and propel people forward. A productive conversation can be critical while still coming from a place of positivity and happiness.

> ***"Even when you're happy, you can still have tough conversations."***

"My hope is that my legacy is really subtle, that I gently and positively encouraged others to be happier or to be more open to admiring happiness. On a bigger scale, I hope that my family and friends know that I operate from a place of happiness. Even when you're happy, you can still have tough conversations. You can still be there to support people through tough situations.

I met with someone last week who, since I left my former job, said so many positive things about my influence and more long-term impact. One of the legacies I left, that I think is amazing, is that the team felt when they met with me that I was always present – they never felt that I was thinking about the next phone call or the next email. I listened. There were other kind examples including that I would say good morning to everyone and that I knew everyone's names. I knew their dogs' and cats' name. It feels good to know that the legacy I left was that people felt heard and they felt safe to share what they had to say. Sometimes the smallest things make the biggest difference, so I don't know so much that I'm necessarily leaving a legacy. I hope my happiness legacy is almost invisible. I'd prefer it be something so subtle or intuitive."

> *"As much as I may feel I'm accountable for my own happiness, the leader has a massive impact on your ability to be your best self, to feel safe, to feel trust, so you can be exactly who you are."*

Fiona does feel that we are each responsible for our own happiness but alluded that when people are unhappy and leave, it's usually because of their boss, and not the job. For leaders who are eager to increase happiness among their staff, high visibility and connection is key. Fiona says she often hears people say, "I never see my leader; my leader knows nothing about me; I'm not sure they even know my name," which leads to employees feeling unimportant or undervalued. Leaders have the greatest impact on the experience of their employees, so it's crucial to make authentic connections with employees and to understand what motivates individuals to be their best self.

Fiona discussed a time when a new leader quickly made it clear to her during a candid conversation that they were not pro-employee. The leader did not recognize the value in having open communication and in building trust with employees. Fiona realized her ability to do her work while staying true to her own values of happiness and integrity would be compromised, so she made some difficult decisions. This was a more extreme circumstance in Fiona's career, but she said when there is conflict or low morale in a workplace, it's important to try to influence where you can be a positive role model. This may involve having those tough conversations to get to the root of why there is so much unhappiness. It's also about knowing when you can't influence and need to move on.

> *"I think as an employee it's important to recognize that you have a fair amount of influence in your day-to-day, and not resign yourself to think that you don't have influence."*

Fiona recognizes that when you do operate from a place of happiness, it can be difficult to be in negative environments, but ultimately, we are responsible for our own happiness and every individual has the power to influence their own mood at work. Even if you feel you are stuck in a job you don't enjoy, or have a boss with whom you don't necessarily see eye-to-eye, it's important to recognize that you still have a fair bit of control over your happiness, and to do your best to exert that control. Sometimes this means waking up in the morning and consciously asking yourself questions such as, "what's the best frame of mind I can have about this situation?" or, "what can I do differently today than I did yesterday?" For Fiona, one thing she's always done to balance her happiness is continuing to produce; when she has a deadline, she meets it. When she's made a commitment, she keeps it.

"It shows that as much as you bring happiness to the workplace, you also bring results. If you can show a balance between the two, that's when you can see some cool stuff happen."

It's not always possible to have the positive influence in the workplace that you'd like, so on a more micro scale, Fiona is a huge proponent for making even small adjustments to your day-to-day life that bring you more joy, such as decorating your space to suit you or bringing more greenery to the office. "One of the things that made me happy in the workplace was bringing a pair of slippers into my office and wearing them. I took off my heels and if I didn't have anywhere to go for a meeting, I wore my slippers. Sometimes it's the small, weird things that can bring you so much joy."

Whether it's wearing slippers in the office, saying good morning, or making authentic connections with people, Fiona is a wonderful example of how happiness can always be brought to the workplace, even when it means having tough conversations.

BEING A POSITIVE LEADER
Creating happiness through kindness
- Bill's story -

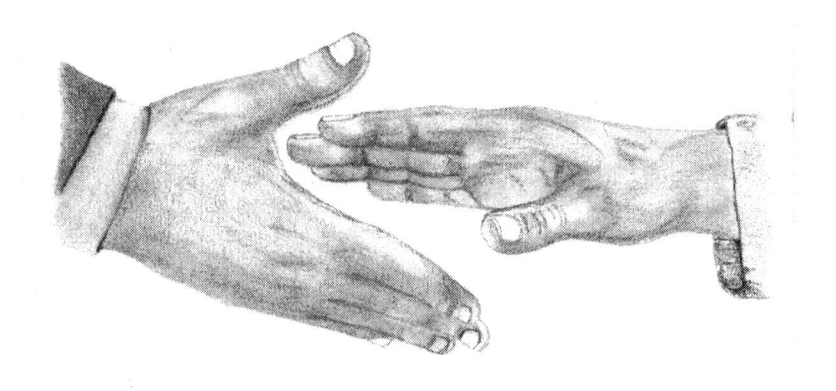

Happiness at work looks different to everyone; it can be about the money, the environment or the nature of the job, but a consistent factor I've noticed among everyone I find to be especially happy at work is their relationships with others. When considering how people are treated, and the role kindness plays in the workplace, I had to talk to my friend, Bill Crawley.

I met Bill in 2006 when he gave me a contract to deliver some of the leadership training that was taking place at the media company where he works. Working with Bill was a pleasure;

he's incredibly bright and professional, but most importantly, he is one of the kindest people I've ever met. What really struck me about Bill was how willing he was to help people; he loved the coaching component of training and making sure that people were given opportunities to grow in their positions. When I began the training, we usually facilitated the sessions as a pair, but once he became the company's Training Manager, Bill passed much of the session work off to me. When I'm doing training with their employees, whenever I mention Bill's name, people can't help but speak about him with so much respect. Even through changes and turbulence in the company, Bill is someone who remains optimistic, and always shows kindness to his colleagues and employees.

> ***"When I know I'm making a difference and feeling that what I do not only makes a difference but is appreciated, that is what motivates me."***

"Generally, I believe people who are happier at work are more authentic, more committed and more driven to work by a true desire to make a difference. They feel that their contribution means something. When I know I'm making a difference and feeling that what I do not only makes a difference but is appreciated, that is what motivates me. That doesn't always come from a boss or someone higher up. It comes from someone you're working with who takes the time to say "thank you."

Bill has been in the newspaper business since 1978 when he got his first job while attending college. After getting married to his first wife and having his first child, he found a fulltime job where he was quickly promoted. "I went from being an office boy for the entire office to being a newspaper advertising salesperson, thanks to the ad director I was working for. He really motivated me and gave me the tools I needed to move up. Back then, the dailies had a hierarchy and it could take six years to get to the top sales salary level, and he took me from nothing to the top level in 12 months, so I worked really, really hard for him."

Bill continued in various Sales Manager and Director roles on the East Coast for several years before moving to Ontario. He took an Advertising Director's job in Northern Ontario which eventually turned into a regional level job. Bill then moved to Simcoe and had a Regional Advertising Director's job for several daily newspapers in the area. When things started to change at the management level, Bill had a conversation with the President of his current company, a mass media publishing company operating primarily in Southern Ontario, and decided to join them. Bill started as a sales trainer which was his role for about three months before taking over training and development. He is now Manager of Learning and Development.

> *"I believe most people like happy people. The only ones that truly don't like happy people are the ones that are not happy themselves."*

"When you are acting in step with who you are, people open to you. When you truly care and respect the people you work with, it's easier to laugh and enjoy each other's company;

that's when the magic happens. I've always said, when you enter a department or business, check the pulse of the room. Is everyone having fun and enjoying the experience? If so, I'll wager they are more successful than a counterpart without the same type of atmosphere.

As for admiration or judgement, I choose admiration. People want to be part of something. When they see a team working together toward common goals, trusting each other, and lifting each other, it is amazing. I have been a part of several teams throughout my career that functioned this way and they were not only the most successful, but hold some of my fondest memories and long-term friendships. I believe most people like happy people. The only ones that truly don't like happy people are the ones that are not happy themselves."

> *"You don't work for a company, you work for, and with, people."*

"I am totally responsible for my happiness. I choose to decide how outside stimuli affect me. It can be tough when you're hearing a lot of negativity, but you must take time to reflect and put things into perspective. "It's the personal relationships that really matter. You don't work for a company; you work for, and with, people. If that is your focus, you can find the motivation to work for them and be part of something more rewarding. If I thought I just worked for a company, and not people, then there is going to be a disconnect.

I think happiness is a choice. I grew up in a tough circumstance, but when I look back, my inclination is to think about the best of times. What you say and think to yourself defines happiness for you. Ghandi says, 'happiness is when what you think, what you say and what you do are in harmony.' If I sit around and think about how bad things are, things are going to be bad, but if I think about and appreciate the good things, it is not so bad."

> *"Having fun and laughing is key to being successful in your role regardless of competence or drive."*

"I had taken on a senior role in a division for a company that was really struggling. One of my biggest weaknesses is the confidence I have that I can change things and motivate people in any circumstance. In this role, I was unable to change the culture that permeated from the highest leadership right to the bottom. I couldn't work in a culture that treated people the way they treated people so badly. I remember observing people in other jobs; I watched how happy they were. I sat down and had a frank conversation with my wife, indicating just how unhappy I truly was. I began looking for something else, which in hindsight probably hastened my departure. The lesson: having fun and laughing is key to being successful in your role regardless of competence or drive. You could be the greatest person in the world, but if you're not in an environment where you're happy, you're going to be miserable and it will affect your personal life. In this case, I was in a world where the culture was going to eat me alive, so I chose to move on and find something else."

"My advice to those wanting to build happier teams is to open up and listen. You can't be happy if you don't like the people you work with, but you may not really know them, so try to get to know them first. As to the company that you work for, if they don't respect you, value you, or give you the opportunity to progress, it may be time for a change."

Bill also suggested that people need to prioritize having a healthy balance between work and personal time, so that their personal life is not so greatly affected by matters concerning their work life. "We spend most of our lives at work, but yet our closest relationships we spend less time with. I know what it's like to drive home and be exhausted and not be able to take my dogs for a walk, or spend time reading to my daughter. I read with my older daughters every night faithfully, and sometimes I really need to challenge myself to do that with my youngest daughter. It's finding the time for the moments that matter. People that are really happy have a better balance for that."

Bill suggested that organizations should ensure their employees know that they are a part of a bigger picture and not just a necessary cog. Employers should offer, not assign, responsibility while setting clear goals. Give your employees the tools for success, along with mutual evaluation on progress, and they will amaze you.

"Some call it coaching but I think it's just listening..."

"I would like to think that people would remember me as someone who cared about them; someone who made a personal connection, even if it was brief. I've been fortunate to have met thousands of people through my various training and development roles through the years and take pride in all the people who have reached out and continue to contact me so many years after working together. Some call it coaching but I think it's just listening, caring and thinking that I can be of assistance. I guess that's what makes me happy – thinking that I can help someone."

Bill is an excellent example not only of what it means to create and maintain happiness for yourself, but what it means to be a leader in the workplace, and how those two things go hand-in-hand. Being happy at work is important, but equally important is being kind, and how that kindness translates to creating happiness for those around us.

REMEMBER THAT LIFE IS GOOD
Shift to a mindset of gratitude
- Karen's story –

There are people you meet throughout your career that seem to bring out the best in others, and it's more challenging not to feel happy when they're around because of their seemingly intrinsic optimism. This was exactly my feeling when I met my good friend, Karen Schmidt.

I met Karen more than 30 years ago while we were working in different departments for the same federally run government organization. We worked together for roughly a year before she left to work for another organization, and we have kept in touch ever since. She truly is optimism personified – even throughout some significant career challenges, she has always maintained a positive outlook at work and in life.

> ***"Happiness at work is when you're not just doing the same thing over and over again – you're being given the opportunity to be entrepreneurial."***

"It's hard to nail down what it means to be happy at work, so I think I have to use a variety of different words: feeling respected, valued, good co-workers, positive management, appreciated and as though you're able to contribute and have variety in your position. Happiness at work is when you're not just doing the same thing over and over again – you're being given the opportunity to be entrepreneurial. It's when you have an opportunity to add value to your tasks and work is a place where you like to be. You never wake up dreading that you have to be somewhere; it's always that you wake up with a sense of gratitude that you get to be there."

Karen has spent most of her career in the not-for-profit sector. Upon the completion of her degree from Brock University, she began working at Canada Employment Centre for Students and eventually accepted a position with the Business Education Council where she did some employment counselling and additional email database work. With more than two decades with the organization, Karen experienced working in a variety of roles, all of which involved helping people and forming meaningful connections. When her relationship with the BEC ended, she took a position with another organization, which for her, ended up being a lesson on the importance of mindfulness when taking on certain opportunities. The job focused heavily on the internal workings of the organization with little room for making connections with people which has always been something she enjoys. Eventually she found her way back to the not-for-profit sector in Beamsville. Being in the not-for-profit sector allowed Karen plenty of opportunities to be creative and entrepreneurial in her approach to problem solving, which was a much more appropriate role. Karen is a wonderful brainstormer – she's one of my go-to people for creative ideas. Through connections she made throughout her career, Karen has spent the past five years working for a regional children's services organization.

> *"As you go through life, it's interesting when things pop up and you come across people, because you're able to flip through the mental rolodex to make the connection that the person you're speaking with would be really great with someone you've met previously."*

For as long as I've known Karen, she has always excelled at making meaningful connections with and for people. Every once in a while, she'll say to me, "you need to meet this person," and more often than not, I develop some type of working relationship with the individual that is beneficial for both of us. During our conversation, she joked that making connections might be her superpower, and I tend to agree with her. To Karen, everyone is interesting in their own way, with their own unique story and talents. Once she meets them, she can immediately make connections to people she has previously met based on their shared experiences or their unique needs. She can recall several occasions where she's run into someone and can remember them right away, though they may not always remember her. She keeps the connections she makes in a mental catalogue of sorts, not with the intention of using them at a later time, but because of her genuine interest in the uniqueness of each person. Whatever they do and however they behave is how you can make and remember the connection. "As you go through life, it's interesting when things pop up and you come across people, because you're able to flip through the mental rolodex to make the connection that the person you're speaking with would be really great with someone you've met previously."

This innate quality that Karen has allows her to make the right connections so that people are able to benefit from each other's skills or experiences. "It's just trying to get people together to see the value in each other and see ways that you can work smarter by working in partnership, rather than parallel to each other."

> ***"You must choose to take the high road and live your true self."***

"When you're always happy or you're always optimistic, people often don't think it's genuine, and think that nobody is truly that happy all the time. I think it depends on the individual and it's probably a reflection of their own happiness. If they think that happiness is not genuine, maybe it's because they've never felt that way themselves. As to whether or not it garners admiration or judgement, you just have to be true to yourself and lead by example, understanding that you will always come across judgmental people. You must choose to take the high road and live your true self."

> ***"Ultimately, it comes down to the individual. There are a lot of reasons to be happy with varying factors."***

"There's a spectrum of optimism, and there's also a spectrum of happiness. I think people are at different points along that spectrum depending on the day and depending on what's happening at home. Everyone has a certain degree of happiness at work but it may not always be directly about work, but I think it's a whole spectrum that depends on the day. The working environment has a lot to do with where people might find themselves on that spectrum: did the cafeteria have the right soup that day? Did someone tell you that you're doing a good job? Is the atmosphere comfortable? Is it a tangible thing? Or is it that your work is being acknowledged? Much of the environment is influenced by the management; if management is choosing to be happy and empowering, then their employees will pick up on that, especially if they feel valued and heard. Ultimately, it comes down to the individual. There are a lot of reasons to be happy with varying factors."

> **"I found the thing I could control is how I responded, and I always chose to respond positively."**

"After reading the *Life is Good* book, and having it reiterated at the training session I attended, I learned that you must shift your mindset. If I was going to tell someone how to build their happiness, I would tell them to try to shift the mindset of the team into thinking that they have opportunities rather than obligations. One woman in the training said rather than saying, 'I have to pick my son up from day-care," she said, "no, I get to. I get to see my mom who is watching him; I get to have a son; I get to have a vehicle that gets me there; I get the opportunity to do all of this.' Even when it's little things you don't necessarily enjoy, shifting your mindset sets you on track to being happier about the choices you're making.

I found the thing I could control is how I responded, and I always chose to respond positively. My own example, and I still feel proud when I look back on it, when all of the shifting and reorganizing happened after 20 years of employment, it felt like such a shock. I went away for the weekend and came back on Monday, knowing I only had four weeks left and I chose to wear my shirt that said, "half-full." There's new challenges and opportunities that will pop up, it just may not feel like it at the time. I'm fortunate to have a lot of things in my life to balance the unhappy moments. Having supportive family and friends will help during those challenging times. Sometimes it's as simple as looking for something good that's happening, or simply having a quote on the wall that feels empowering to you." Karen later added that having good friends who are like minded and supportive feeds the positivity and helps keep the optimism alive.

> *"I always choose to see the optimistic side of life. I always choose to look at the glass as more than half full because life is just better that way."*

"I think that leading by example is an important legacy to leave. If you choose to be positive and you respect people while treating them well, then that example will resonate with others. I believe there's always a positive side to every situation and that there is always something to learn. You can only control how you react."

"I always choose to see the optimistic side of life. I always choose to look at the glass as more than half full because life is just better that way. I don't know that I've ever not felt optimistic. It's just a part of my nature, but I also find that you can cultivate it a bit more in how you choose to display that optimism in certain situations or at work. There are always things that are negative, but you need to decide how you will react to those situations. You can always choose to see the positive side of things. It's intuitive for me to respond to things in an optimistic way."

Over the years, Karen and I have continued volunteering together and she is one of the reasons that I became invested in learning more about what makes people happy at work. "When you are more positive and optimistic, it seems to attract similar people. I would say that most of my good friends are optimistic people. It seems like we are able to find as well as support each other, and that positivity builds."

OWN IT, WORK IT & LIVE IT
Take charge of your personal & professional development
- *Kevin's story* –

I met Kevin Farrelly while facilitating a four-day leadership training program at a local technology company. During each learning day, a leader from the organization would speak about their leadership journey with the group. Listening to each speaker tell their story about what brought them to become a leader at the company was the highlight of the program for everyone, myself included. Kevin spoke frequently over the course of the four days, and each time it was clear that he loved his job. While catching up with Kevin, it is evident that through all the changes Kevin has seen in the company and himself, his happiness in the workplace has never wavered.

> *"As I look at the different things I've done, whenever I'm learning, growing, or getting better than I was yesterday is when I'm happiest."*

"For me, happiness is a couple of things: definitely the ability to grow personally. As I look at the different things I've done, whenever I'm learning, growing, or getting better than I was yesterday is when I'm happiest. That was reinforced when I moved to this role from operations to training manager, not that I wasn't learning in the old role, but the amount of learning increased and really brought me a lot of joy. Growing personally and adding value to the company and others is a key factor for me. I've really started to embrace that as my personal motto. As I studied and researched happiness, it was exciting to see that what I was doing was adding up to some of the theories. Even though I didn't realize it was part of the theory, those two things have stuck out in my mind as key indicators for happiness in the workplace."

> *"I still have ambition but I'm not thinking I've got to be doing this without enjoying what I'm currently doing. That's the contentment piece."*

"I would say over the last 10 years, making myself and my employees happy has definitely been done mindfully. As part of my personal development, it's been on the forefront. It's something that I work on for myself and for others. For example, when I had a larger direct report team, we were creating opportunities for people to challenge themselves and problem solve, which I believe helps with their personal development. People seem to be happier when they're contributing and solving problems. For myself, again, I've got a couple thoughts here: happiness is being content but never satisfied. I've come across that in some readings, but, as I've really started to understand the difference between the two, where I'm happy to be doing what I'm doing but I'm not really satisfied. I still have ambition but I'm not thinking I've got to be doing this without enjoying what I'm currently doing. That's the contentment piece."

Kevin started in 1995 as a frontline technician. He prepared himself for new opportunities by taking home the company manuals to familiarize himself so that he would have a thorough understanding of their products. As supervisory positions became available, Kevin was in an excellent position, having the necessary knowledge to take on more responsibility within the company. He applied for various supervisor positions that became available internally, and although the opportunities were not immediately given to him, he was still seen as a leader in his department thanks to his proactive approach in learning all that he could about the company and its products.

> *"It's important to give people opportunities to find the sweet spot outside of their comfort zone, but not so far outside of their comfort zone that they're stressed."*

Kevin considers himself fortunate to have had the career he has had and believes himself to be generally happy on a daily basis. His belief is that while the leadership of a workplace can be an influencing factor on an employee's happiness, ultimately, happiness is an internal piece for which we are individually responsible. That is not to say that once it has been achieved, it's there to stay; happiness for Kevin involves continuing to grow and always being better than he was the day before. When he moved from his position as a supervisor to a training manager, his learning increased which brought more joy to his professional and personal life. Maintaining and increasing happiness at work happens when he is growing and adding value to the company. He believes the same logic should be applied when managing talent within an organization, that people should always be left better than they are found. Kevin has often supported people from his team to move to new roles within the company because they were so passionate about wanting to grow. It has been equally important to facilitate transitions when people are no longer fit for the role they have currently. One particular instance involved Kevin facilitating a move for an employee who was struggling in the role they currently had. The employee was incredibly unhappy and reluctant about the transition but was afterwards grateful and has since gone on to do great things in the company. As a leader, recognizing and understanding how and where talent should be used within an organization is an important piece for creating and maintaining a happy workplace.

Over the course of the past decade, Kevin has been more mindful about happiness for himself and trying to create happiness for others around him. When he was in a management role, he was conscious about creating opportunities for his team to solve problems within the department. Not only does this help with development, but Kevin believes that when people are able to contribute and challenge themselves in meaningful ways that impact the organization, they are happier. He is also more aware of how people must be challenged to optimize efficiency for the company and overall employee happiness when he's setting up employees on a team. "It's important to give people opportunities to find the sweet spot outside of their comfort zone, but not so far outside of their comfort zone that they're stressed. Stress can be good for growth, but it can be to the point where it's too much and now someone hates their job because maybe it's gone too far. If they're doing mundane work and not being challenged, they might be very unhappy, so you want to pull and stretch, but be aware that any pendulum can swing too far." Throughout his career, Kevin has seen several leadership styles and how they can impact the employees around them, and ultimately the leaders like him who want to make a difference in other people are happier themselves with typically happier teams. Taking responsibility to ensure we are becoming better each day, and leaving people better than we found them, will affect not only an individual's personal growth but their happiness as well.

"Time flies when you enjoy what you're doing, when you're not a clock watcher."

"I think the value to having happiness in the workplace is personal satisfaction. This is a win-win; your quality and quantity of work are affected by your happiness at work so that's going to be good for the organization and good for the individual. Time flies when you enjoy what you're doing, when you're not a clock watcher. Again, the 25 years I've been here feel like a light second. It's coming from engaging, challenging, exciting work. When you're bored or unhappy, time just seems to go backwards. I think that would be the value of having happiness at work."

"Own it, work it, live it"

"I've seen people that are happy in an environment that is clearly not the greatest, or who have a boss that isn't the greatest, but they're finding ways to manage it. They're still seeing the good in things."

This is one of the mottos Kevin follows when it comes to happiness at work and a legacy he hopes to leave at his workplace. He believes that we are responsible for our own happiness and that no one else can make us feel a certain way. His ability and track record of navigating through growth and challenges in the workplace over the course of his career has given him the opportunity to practice owning and taking responsibility for his own happiness. Though he can boast about being generally happy throughout his career, Kevin acknowledges that it has not always been joyful. While he was still working as a Production Manager, Kevin said that he often would not experience joy in his job until the quarter was over and everything had been shipped successfully. The pressure and daily grind of ensuring production was running efficiently often resulted in three long months at a time of not experiencing joy. It was at this point where Kevin realized that he needed to incorporate other motivators.

> *"The important thing is knowing when to get out of the rut and to not stay for too long because that is when it becomes a grave."*

Kevin realized it was the daily wins that needed to be acknowledged in order to get through the days when the quarter was going by slowly. The daily wins usually involved acknowledging whether his daily impact while coaching staff was good or constructive. By making this slight adjustment, to acknowledge smaller, daily wins, Kevin was able to remain motivated and invigorated in his job for years to follow. Kevin's change in attitude is one example of an individual owning and being responsible for their own happiness in the workplace. Acknowledging daily wins is a process Kevin put in place for himself to ensure he was kept content in his professional life.

Owning, working and living happiness may also involve actively researching and studying what happiness is to better understand what it is that needs to be achieved. It may not be as simple as finding a job you love and being happy every day. It may involve creating processes for yourself the way Kevin did by acknowledging small, daily wins. Turning off the buzzer on his smartphone was another process he found necessary for his happiness at work since he found the buzzing to be associated only with bad news, such as a shipment not going through. It's also been five years since Kevin has watched the news which he says has been critical to maintaining his overall happiness. He still gets his news through other sources but says that no longer watching the news has made a huge difference in his life. For Kevin, just as important as creating happiness at work is for the individual to not be hard on themselves when they have had a bad day, or a few bad days. Being happy at work is not synonymous with being thrilled to be at work every second of every day. Some days are harder than others and it is okay to not be happy all the time. The important thing is knowing when to get out of the rut and to not stay for too long because that is when it becomes a grave.

It is not very often that a person stays with a company for such a huge portion of their career, but Kevin's happiness journey taking place over the course of 25 years with one company shows that it is possible to be happy in one place for a long time. Sometimes, being happy at one place means maneuvering through different levels of the company and sometimes, even taking a pay cut to truly follow a passion. Engaging, challenging and exciting work is what has given Kevin so much joy throughout his career, but that did not involve staying stagnant in one position for too long.

Kevin recently moved on to a smaller local company that is looking to grow. He looks back on the past 25 years fondly, but as a continuous learner, is looking forward to a new adventure where he can bring his experience to help them mature their people and processes, as well as bring the same methods of instilling happiness in the workplace.

SERVE OTHERS WITH A SMILE
Finding happiness by bringing happiness to others
- Barb's story –

When eating at a restaurant, the server can really enhance or diminish your dining experience based on their level of service. With Barb Kovacs as your server, you are guaranteed outstanding service and will leave the restaurant feeling like family.

I met Barb a few years ago at a restaurant in the Long Beach area of Wainfleet, Ontario, not at all far from where I live. My husband and I find ourselves there regularly for special occasions and quite often on the evenings we would prefer not to cook. The year I met Barb, she happened to be our server quite often and was always phenomenal. She got to know us so well that she knew our preferences in food and would have our drink orders ready at our table before we even sat down. She was always personable and could continue our conversation from the last time we had the pleasure of having her as our server. While we've always enjoyed having Barb as a server for her pleasant demeanour and commitment to quality service, what impressed me most was the time my husband and I went to the restaurant to celebrate our anniversary and she remembered from the year before. November came around and we found ourselves there once again. The restaurant staff came over with a cheesecake and sang happy birthday to me; she remembered that from the year before as well. I asked her how it is she can do that, and her response was simply, "it's just something that I do. I remember things; I remember people; I remember events." This is the kind of service she provides to all of her customers.

Serving is a difficult, physically demanding job; it requires a lot of late hours and sometimes dealing with difficult people. The burnout and turnover rate in the industry is high, but Barb is dedicated to creating a positive customer experience, and it has always seemed to come naturally to her. I knew that people could benefit from her perspective and was able to learn more about how she has brought happiness into her work.

> ***"For me, it doesn't matter if I'm serving the same food every day, or serving the same people every day, as long as I'm mentally or physically engaged, that is when I'm happiest."***

"Happiness at work for me is how engaged I am in the job. Serving allows me to engage with people, and often it is people that I like which is helpful. It helps with my happiness, but we are responsible for that happiness as well. To be able to find happiness at work is a personal thing, and you have the choice as to whether you're going to be happy at work or not. Sometimes it requires a conscious effort to think about that decision and to be mindful of it. You must work hard at it, otherwise it may be time to move on. I think a lot of people feel that they are stuck or that they have no have other options. If I find that I am not happy somewhere, I ask myself what will my next step be? For me, it doesn't matter if I'm serving the same food every day, or serving the same people every day, as long as I'm mentally or physically engaged, that is when I'm happiest."

Barb began her serving career with her first job at a restaurant in downtown Welland. She continued working at the restaurant in tandem with several other jobs, all while attending college fulltime. It was at this point that Barb really began realizing how much she loved working with and serving people. She recently left the restaurant in Wainfleet and has since taken a position working at an upscale restaurant overlooking Lake Ontario in the Niagara Region. She was quickly promoted to a supervisory role as management immediately recognized her enthusiasm and dedication. Her balanced approach of hard work and personality makes her one of the best servers I have ever had the pleasure of meeting, and it's clear to everyone she serves that she loves what she does.

Once Barb had her daughter, Emma, life immediately became about taking care of and providing for her. Barb was working as a manager at a country club in Port Colborne at the time but was regularly working up to 80 hours per week; her father would bring Emma to the golf course on Sundays just so Barb would have a chance to see her. As Emma got older, Barb realized that working so many hours was not conducive to raising a child. She transitioned to a serving job at a chain restaurant, where the hours were not as many, but the late nights made it difficult to see her daughter once again. She was able to take on an administrative role where she worked for seven years. The job gave her a better work-life balance; she was able to work during the day and be home in the evenings and on weekends. Through those seven years, she still took on a few serving roles, including her job in Wainfleet, for the extra income and because she still had so much passion for serving people and making those connections. "Through serving, I've always met such interesting people. I ended up working with a gentleman who had a business that ensured that we keep honeybees safe; it was an interesting experience. I also helped my friend who owns a vending machine business which was a cool job. I was on the road a lot but got to meet a lot of people when I was making deliveries. I'm drawn to jobs because there's something interesting about them. Serving has always been about that interaction with people, but in other jobs I've had, including administrative support, it's been a new challenge for me, which is something that has always kept me going."

Barb worked at our local restaurant in Wainfleet as a server for nearly 12 years, during which she found herself a secondary job in a supervisory role. She worked there for roughly five years, and though she enjoyed the challenges brought by the new experience, she wasn't able to interact with people as often as she did when serving, which is the aspect of serving she loves most.

Where others require consistency and security in their work life, Barb has always been able to transition between jobs when she feels she has outgrown the experience. "I'm happiest when I don't feel caged or tethered. I say that with anything, whether it's a relationship or work. I definitely require having some freedom and I think that's why I don't mind working so much. At one point I had four jobs on the go at once because they were all different and allowed me some freedom. I find when I outgrow something that I'm always looking for the next thing. I don't think I'll ever be the person to spend her life in one career."

> ***"There's always a way to reward people and show them that you value their work."***

"If you want to make your team happier, you have to engage with them and really get to know the people that work for you. You should not see them as expendable or just another face. There's always a way to reward people and show them that you value their work."

Much of Barb's career has been spent in supervisor or managerial roles where her responsibility has involved maintaining a positive morale among other employees. In order to ensure people are happy at work, Barb believes that there are responsibilities from both the employee and the employer. "I think you need to have a positive mindset going in. If you're not happy in your job, then maybe it's time to find something else. I also think there's responsibility on the employer's side; I don't want to work for someone that is miserable all the time because that will inevitably affect employees and the workplace. It's easy to say you won't let someone else affect your behaviour or emotions, but when someone around you is miserable all the time, it can be difficult. Even when you know you're doing a good job, it's necessary to have your employer let you know that they value that hard work, and that it's not for nothing."

In Barb's supervisory role, she understood the responsibility she had to her employees to keep them happy in their work, but also understood that the employees had a responsibility to improve their own experience at work. "I have employees that I value so much because of their capabilities to go above and beyond. I try to be fair to all of them, but the ones that really put the work in might get an extra shift or a better suite; sometimes it's just the little things that count."

> *"If somebody else can get something from my happiness, that is the value I see in being happy at work."*

"Happiness spreads to other people. People often ask at the restaurant if I'm serving that night, so I know I've left a positive impact. If somebody else can get something from my happiness, that is the value I see in being happy at work. I've been in the food and beverage industry for quite a few years because there's something about it that I like. I sort of get to take care of people. I definitely see the value in knowing that someone can walk about and think 'that was a really good experience.' I find that when people come back, customers I've previously served may not specifically ask for me, but they want me to stop by their table to talk. That's the value for me. It's just making other people happy."

When Barb was still serving in Wainfleet, based on her dedication and her ability to connect with us and so many other customers, I told her that she should be training everyone in the restaurant. She told me as much as she would love to, her number one priority was the dining experience for her customers. We miss seeing her at our local restaurant on those special occasions but are thrilled for the people who will experience her service wherever she ends up.

Final thoughts...

I am eternally grateful to the 10 wonderful individuals featured in this book for their willingness to share their ideas along with such personal experiences so freely and candidly. Although these ten people come from different professional backgrounds with their own unique perspectives, I noticed some common themes throughout the interviews and while putting the book together.

The individuals interviewed are all very self-aware of themselves and how their decisions can affect their personal happiness as well as the happiness of the people they interact with in their respective workplaces. Being self-aware allows people to recognize what they have control over, as well as what they do not, and how they will allow these factors to influence their own decisions or overall happiness.

All of the interviewees are lifelong learners yearning for more information and to continue perfecting their craft. They are the people who take assessments, and are open to criticism, in order to gain a higher understanding of their personal strengths and areas for improvement. They take the time to reflect on their happiness and their goals. They recognize when changes are needed to maintain that happiness, whether it is making small changes, or taking a giant leap.

Each of the people in this book have high levels in Daniel Goleman's 4 Domains of Emotional Intelligence: self-awareness, self-management, social awareness, and relationship management. As much as they recognize that how they conduct themselves is crucial to their workplace happiness, they are also sensitive to the needs of others. They genuinely want others to be happy and will do everything in their power to ensure the success of others.

They also have an unwavering hold on their personal values; they recognize what is important to them and they base their decisions around those values.

When navigating change in their workplace, all of the individuals are able to do it with great flexibility and optimism; many of them seek out change when something is not working, and they want to maintain their happiness.

Lastly, and possibly, most importantly, they are joyful. They bring laughter to their everyday and to their teams. They recognize that even though there can be tough situations that must be overcome, happiness is a choice to be made each day.

Based on the lessons I've learned from the 10 people in the book, as well as others I've encountered through my career who are happy at work, I've created an acronym for happiness that can help others with their own happiness journeys.

An acronym for Happiness:

Have a good sense of self

Appreciate the uniqueness in everyone

Passion is crucial and leads to a positive, collaborative culture

Playfulness should play a role in the workday

Inspect your own values often

Navigate change with flexibility and optimism

Emotionally intelligent people are happier and more resilient

Serve others including your peers, staff, clients and community

See the good in each day

Thank you for taking the time to read the stories outlined in this book. I hope it will help with your own workplace happiness and how you can bring that same happiness to your teams.

Are you a happy leader?

Answer the questions used during the interviews for this book. Visit **https://bit.ly/3jCq2cM** to download a copy of the questionnaire and see for yourself or visit sandrasummerhayes.com to see how I can help you and your team become happier at work.

ABOUT THE AUTHOR

Sandra's mission is to help leaders succeed and she has been doing that her entire career which began as an Employment Counsellor and Workshop Facilitator with Human Resources Development Canada. After her 12-year tenure, she was hired as part of Casino Niagara's pre-opening Management team where she managed the Training Department for 3 years. In 1999, she started her own Training & Development company where she has designed and facilitated experiential training for many organizations across Canada. Sandra has also worked with organizational supervisors and managers to develop individual learning plans to strengthen their leadership abilities. Sandra has also been a keynote speaker for several conferences.

Sandra is a Master Trainer, Certified Training Professional, Certified Laughter Leader, Certified Coach Practitioner and one of only 3 Thiagi Certified Trainers in Canada. She also holds certifications in Teaching Adults, Human Resources, Level 3 Personality Dimensions® Master Trainer, the Myers Briggs Type Indicator®, Emotional Intelligence and DISC®.

Sandra grew up in Port Colborne and now lives on the sunny shores of Lake Erie in Wainfleet, Ontario with her awesome husband (and illustrator of this book) Chris. For more information on what Sandra can do for you and your team, please visit: www.sandrasummerhayes.com.

Manufactured by Amazon.ca
Bolton, ON